A Patriot's Memoirs
of World War II

Through my eyes, heart, and soul

LUCIANO "LOUIS" CHARLES GRAZIANO

LifeRich
PUBLISHING®

Scriptures taken from the Holy Bible, New International Version®, NIV®. Copyright © 1973, 1978, 1984, 2011 by Biblica, Inc.™ Used by permission of Zondervan. All rights reserved worldwide. www.zondervan.com The "NIV" and "New International Version" are trademarks registered in the United States Patent and Trademark Office by Biblica, Inc.™

LifeRich Publishing is a registered trademark of The Reader's Digest Association, Inc.

LifeRich Publishing books may be ordered through booksellers or by contacting:

LifeRich Publishing
1663 Liberty Drive
Bloomington, IN 47403
www.liferichpublishing.com
1 (888) 238-8637

ISBN: 978-1-4897-2048-1 (sc)
ISBN: 978-1-4897-2050-4 (hc)
ISBN: 978-1-4897-2049-8 (e)

Library of Congress Control Number: 2018968003

Print information available on the last page.

LifeRich Publishing rev. date: 12/21/2018

Credits and Acknowledgments—images taken from:

- Friends of the National World War II Memorial
- The McDuffie Progress
- The National Museum of the US Army
- The *VFW* magazine
- WWII Veterans Committee
- *American Valor Quarterly* magazine
- National Mounted Warfare Foundation
- The Eisenhower Foundation
- Mary Jean Eisenhower, the granddaughter of General Eisenhower
- Helen Denton, Dwight D. Eisenhower's personal secretary
- The State Historical Society of Missouri—Photo by the US Army Signal Corps
- T/5 Howard Schnebly
- The National Archives
- Bernard Bennett

This book is dedicated to the memory of the love of my life, Bobbie, my beautiful wife of sixty-two years. We met while we were both serving our country during WWII. We fell in love in France and got married while we were both in the service. Our lives were always busy, with five children (and sometimes foster children), our own business, church, the Knights of Columbus, and the VFW. Bobbie was the first female to serve as a post commander and district commander of the VFW in the state of Georgia. There wasn't much that didn't get done once Bobbie set her mind to it. This contributed to her many accomplishments, both for our family and for any task she undertook. We all miss this very special lady who, through our memories, continues to make us laugh!

CONTENTS

SOLDIER'S CREED

I am an American Soldier.

I am a warrior and a member of a team.

I serve the people of the United States, and live the Army Values.

I will always place the mission first.

I will never accept defeat.

I will never quit.

I will never leave a fallen comrade.

I am disciplined, physically and mentally tough, trained and proficient in my warrior tasks and drills.

I always maintain my arms, my equipment and myself.

I am an expert and I am a professional.

I stand ready to deploy, engage, and destroy, the enemies of the United States of America in close combat.

I am a guardian of freedom and the American way of life.

I am an American Soldier.

THE NATIONAL MUSEUM OF THE U.S. ARMY

2425 Wilson Boulevard, Arlington, Virginia 22201 • www.armyhistory.org

FOREWORD

My father, Luciano "Louis" Charles Graziano, yields himself to God, Who continues to bring out his talents. Dad develops the talents God gives him and gives all the glory to the Lord. My father is a perfect example of the understanding that life is an ongoing process—a gradual growth in grace and in the talents that God has placed within all of us.

Dad never says, "What's the use now? I'm too old. My life is about over." He presses on in his walk with God, realizing that what God has for him was too much to cram into the first eighty-plus years of his life. "There is a time for everything" (Ecc. 3:1, NIV).

In his book, Dad shows that he is a "man of many talents." He paints a beautiful picture for the rest of us to see what God's love for us looks like. He sets a standard for us to live by, and we are so blessed because he is our father. There is a saying, "Respect is earned, and love is given." Dad certainly earns the respect of everyone who knows him. He shows much love to all.

As water reflects a man's face, so his heart reflects the man. Dad has a big heart. He is a generous man, a man of understanding and patience. He is a "take-charge man."

Dad's thoughts of writing his experiences during WWII weighed heavily on his heart for many years. He wanted his family, friends, and other veterans to know what he experienced during this war, so he finally put it all into a book. Now, at the age of ninety-five, he is sharing "the good, the bad, and the ugly."

"The good" begins with a love story that lasted sixty-two years. He met my mother, a fellow soldier, in France during the war, and they married there while still actively serving their country. "The bad and the ugly" tells of Dad's experiences in the war itself.

This book also tells of the unimaginable lessons he learned when his contractor skills were challenged while constructing many types of buildings. With no formal training or experience in this field, Dad relied on the grace of God to complete all the assignments he received.

It's amazing the amount of personal pictures Dad took during his time overseas. We teased and asked him, "Did you carry a camera instead of a gun?" We always wondered why he had so many pictures and later learned that he had a passion for taking pictures long before he ever joined the military. His personal pictures and memorabilia are denoted with an asterisk.

The following memoirs are about a small-town boy who had to grow up quickly at the age of twenty when Uncle Sam drafted him into the army. It tells of his experiences and thoughts and takes you along on his journey to the end of WWII. It is about exhibiting courage and bravery amidst the heartache of the loss of fellow soldiers and friends. It is about having tremendous faith in God and trusting Him. And we who love him are eternally grateful that Dad's faith, trust, and prayers prevailed in getting him back home safely.

I'm so glad Dad decided to share his experiences. I pray that future Americans do not forget about the incredibly brave men who landed on the shores of Normandy to liberate Europe and free the world.

Enjoy your journey with Dad through his military years.

Moira Graziano Johnson

INTRODUCTION

I was born February 6, 1923, and lived in the small town of East Aurora, New York. My parents came over from Sicily, Italy, and were processed at Ellis Island before they settled in East Aurora. My father, Pietro, brought my mother, Filipa, and himself over for a chance at a better life. My father was a hardworking man who loved his family. Being from Italy, they spoke very little English. I can't imagine the hardships they must have endured with the language barrier. One day, my mother needed some eggs. The clerk did not know what she was trying to tell him. She immediately squatted down and started to cluck like a chicken and started to flap her arms like they were wings. He got the picture, and she got her eggs!

I had to quit school and go to work after I finished the eighth grade. Times were hard. My father found work as a railroad watchman, a job that did not require use of the English language. When his night watchman job played out, he found a job as a brick mason. My mother stayed home with the five children—Phyllis, Josephine, Angie, Carmen, and me. I was the youngest of the five. Later, my sister Phyllis opened a beauty salon. My mother, my sister, and my brother became hairstylists. I made the decision to follow in my family's legacy, becoming a hairstylist also.

It was in the cold month of January 1943, when I received a letter from Uncle Sam, ordering me to report to Fort Niagara, New York, for a physical. I knew the United States was at war, but I didn't know what was ahead of me. It was then that I made a promise to Uncle Sam to pick up a gun, put on a helmet, and defend our country with my life. I was honored to do so. My thoughts were then, *I'm ready to go,* never realizing how much my military experience would change the course of my life. The date of my induction into the army was January 22, 1943. My starting pay was $21 a month, with my overseas pay jumping to $185 a month when I made master sergeant. I thought, *Wow! I'm making a lot of money!* Thinking back, it really wasn't, considering I would be putting my life on the line many times. (How far would $185 last in today's economy?)

I found out that three of my buddies were ordered to report to Fort Niagara at the same time I had to go. It was a shame that we all were sent to different places. I never saw them again.

I proudly served my country with no hesitation and no regrets. My brother was also in the army. I made sergeant in eight months and master sergeant in twenty-three months. I am excited to take you on my journey during WWII.

1

My Journey Begins

I was inducted into the United States Army at Fort Niagara, New York, and had an experience in those first few days I will never forget. I loved any challenge thrown at me, because I received much satisfaction in accomplishing whatever came before me—even having to shave off my mustache! One day my captain came to me and told me I had to shave it off, "or else." Well, I did not want to know what "or else" meant, so I shaved it off. I had it for several years and did not feel right without it. I only shaved it that one time before I got transferred out of Fort Niagara. I let it grow back, and no one else ordered me to shave it again. To this day, I have my mustache.

No Mustache*   *Me Today at 95**

After I left Fort Niagara, New York, I was sent to Camp Hood, now known as Fort Hood, in Killeen, Texas. The first day I got there, two other soldiers and I had to peel six bushels of potatoes. The next day, we were put with Company A 138 TDRTC Fourth Brigade for thirteen weeks of combat training. It was tough on me, never having done any physical work. I took all the challenges as they came, not letting anything bother me, even having to run twenty laps around the barracks one morning because I was late for reveille. You can bet your bottom dollar that I was never late again! Working as a hairstylist did not prepare me for what I had to do to get in shape for combat. But I made it. That is just the way I am, ready to take on any challenge that is thrown at me. I love a challenge.

After my thirteen weeks of training, I was sent to Camp Shanks in Orangetown, New York (named for Major General David Carey Shanks) for special training for four more weeks. Then I was sent to Fort Dix, New Jersey, to get ready to go overseas. This was my last stop in the good ol' USA.

The night before I got on the ship, my buddy and I went into the city. I made a record about everything I thought would happen to Mussolini and sent it to my father. Mussolini and Hitler were allies. I talked about Mussolini because he was from Italy like my father. What I predicted came true. After the war, I learned my father played that record all the time. I think it kept him going until I came home.

Mussolini and Hitler

The next morning, we boarded our ship, the *Queen Mary.* Imagine being a boy who had never left his small hometown, boarding a large ship going overseas. I was fearful and anxious, not knowing where we were going or what we were going to encounter.

Queen Mary

There were more than sixteen thousand troops on the ship. There were so many that we had to take turns where we slept—in the bunks one night and on the deck the next.

KEEP THIS CARD 40

SLEEPING QUARTERS

ROOM A 19

Queen Mary

Sleeping Quarters Card
My sleeping quarters card, given to
*me when I boarded the ship.**

I slept in the bunks the first night. It was so tight I could not turn over. We had to get out of the bunk and turn the way we wanted to be and get back in. That was enough for me! I told them I would sleep on deck every night with my lifejacket, just in case we were torpedoed. I slept with my overcoat on and all the blankets I could find. I figured at least I would have a chance if we came under attack. I knew it was very cold, and I learned later that this was the coldest winter in many years.

When we were crossing the ocean, we had to use the zigzag method every six minutes to avoid the German U-boats. Not only did we have to worry about the U-boats, but we were also confronted with a major storm at sea. We were seven hundred miles from Scotland when the *Queen Mary* was suddenly hit broadside by a huge wave. I later learned that wave may have reached a height of ninety-two feet, and it was calculated later that the ship rolled fifty-two degrees. The *Queen Mary* almost turned over, and they told us she would have capsized if she had rolled another three degrees. I knew God was with us.

An account of this crossing can be found in Walter Ford Carter's book, *No Greater Sacrifice, No Greater Love*. Carter's father, Dr. Norval Carter, part of the 110th Station Hospital on board at the time, wrote, "that at one-point Queen Mary damned near capsized." The incident inspired Paul Gallico to write his novel, *The Poseidon Adventure* (1969). This was adapted as a 1972 film by the same name.

They did not tell us where we were going until the third day out at sea. We had to change course because of the German U-boats forcing us to go to Scotland instead of England. It took us about six days to reach Scotland. From there we boarded a train to Camp Weston in England. There, I was put in Headquarters OISE Section Command-Z European Theater of Operations US Army, APO 513 T/3.

2

Eighteen Months in England

We had more combat training at Camp Weston in England. They had two converted DUKWs (a six-wheel-drive amphibious vehicle) parked in an open field with their ladders extended far into the sky and fastened together to form an inverted V. We were lined up single file and had to climb a very shaky ladder, step across very carefully at the top, and descend on the other side. Two of my men froze momentarily midjourney, but everybody made it.

We continued our combat training a few more weeks. Then we had to put up some houses for the many troops coming in for training. The general came in one day and asked me to go to London for a special mission for the army. He said not to tell anyone what he had me to do—*ever!* (FYI, to this day, I have never revealed this classified mission to anyone.) I was there about six weeks and then came back to Camp Weston.

Camp Weston
Picture taken at Camp Weston in England *
I was featured in my local newspaper, The
McDuffie Progress, and shared this photo
with them to use for the write-up.

When I was in London, the Germans would send blitz firebomb raids almost every night, which used the V1 and V2 bombs. They would whistle down and explode, and we never knew where. Nearly twenty thousand bombs had been dropped on London by the Luftwaffe, the aerial warfare branch of the combined German military forces during World War ll. It took the London fire brigade and several of its members to put out the fires caused by the bombs.

I didn't know if I was going to get hit; however, I knew God was with me because of my faith and prayers. There was nothing more terrifying than to hear bombs coming down on us. That put fear in me and made me pray harder to God for protection.

Bombings in London

While I was in London, I was walking down the street and looked across and saw a boy from my hometown, Norman Wittmeyer, walking under Big Ben. I did not know him very well, as he was older than me. You know what they say, "It's a small world." I walked over to him, and we had a good visit. It was really good to see a familiar face from home. That visit boosted my spirits.

After I left London and went back to Camp Weston, Captain Robert H. Wormhoudt sent for me. I went to see him, and he wanted me to take over Utilities, so he made me Utilities-NCO Sergeant.

AN OFFICER AND A GENTLEMAN
CAPT. R. H. WORMHOUDT

Wormhoudt Sketch *
"My Captain"—Robert H. Wormhoudt
A drawing given to me by the artist: T/5 Howard Schnebly
T/5 Howard Schnebly was one of my men.

I oversaw thirty-five utility men, and I supervised them in plumbing, carpentry, electrical work, masonry, road building, and construction work. I assigned them to their jobs and inspected their completed work. Thank goodness for being able to obtain books on how to get all this accomplished. I did a lot of reading.

While I was there, a German plane would come every night to wake us up. We called him "Bedtime Charlie." I told my men to stay up with me one night to get Charlie. They did, and we got him. I had put a tracer bullet (one that lights up) in my gun every fourth bullet to be able to find our target. After the plane went down, we went looking for it and found it. There were two German soldiers in the plane, and they were dead. I got some souvenirs from the plane, and then we went back to camp. I put everything on my desk and went out to the bathroom. When I came back to my office, everything was gone. I guess the boys liked them better than I did. I let it go, because there was no need to question anybody. I knew they would not tell on each other.

The next day, my men and I had to start building a large mess hall at Camp Weston to feed all the troops coming in for more combat training. We put up fifty Nissen huts for the troops to sleep in and built latrines, roads, sidewalks, a power plant for lights, and a theater. I was very glad I had such good efficient men to help me accomplish everything.

Nissen Hut *
One of the Nissen huts I oversaw the building
of, which I used for my quarters.

Louis in front of tent *
Me in front of one of the tents in "Tent City"

We had so many troops coming in that I was put in charge of getting forty tents put up, besides the Nissen huts we built. They called me "Mayor of Tent City." The troops were coming in for their training to get ready for the invasion.

The captain came in one day and told me to put someone in charge of my job. I put Buck Barnette in charge; he was my sidekick.

*Louis and Buck's Sketch ***
Tech Sergeant Louis C. Graziano and Staff Sergeant Earcell
R. Barnett (Buck) of the HQ Command Utilities Center
Another drawing given to me by artist T/5 Howard Schnebly

Wondering why he asked this of me, I went to talk to him. He said he needed me to take over for the barber because he was sick. I said, "How did you know I could cut hair?" He said, "I looked at your papers, and I saw where you were a hairstylist in New York." Well, I changed hats and went to the barbershop. Of all things, the first person I had to cut was the general. I said to myself, "Oh, hell!" But I did all right, and he was pleased. I worked in the barbershop for two weeks. I was glad when I got to get back outside with my men.

W. H. Boshoff, Lieutenant Colonel, GSC, Headquarters Commandant was so impressed with me and the work I had done, that he awarded me with a commendation for my command as Utilities Foreman.

```
                    HEADQUARTERS COMMAND
                    HEADQUARTERS OISE SECTION
                    COM Z  EUROPEAN T OF OPNS
                         U. S. ARMY

                                              APO 513
201.22 - Graziano, Louis (EM)              28 October 1944


SUBJECT:  Commendation

TO     :  Tec 3 Louis Graziano, Hq Co, Hq Oise Sec, APO 513.
          (Thru Company Commander, Hq Co)


     1.  I am much impressed with the value of the work you have done
in this Command as Utilities Foreman.

     2.  Your hours have been long, your help few, material scarce,
and difficulties abundant, but you have done well.  I consider you as
an example to the remainder of your non-commissioned officers.  I find
in you a man who says little, but does much.

     3.  I am proud to have a man of your stamp in my organization,
and I desire you to note that I appreciate what you are doing for me.



                              W. H. BOSHOFF, Lt. Col., GSC,
                              Headquarters Commandant.

201.22 - Graziano, Louis (EM)    1st Ind.                   RHW/rp
HQ. CO., HQ. OISE SECTION, COM Z, EUROPEAN T OF OPNS, APO 513  29 Oct. 44
TO: Tec 3 Louis Graziano, Hq. Co., Hq. Oise Sec. APO 513

     1.  It is with great pleasure that I forward this commendation to you.


                              ROBERT H. WORMHOUDT
                              1st Lt., C.A.C.
                              Commanding



                           - 1 -
```

Utilities Foreman's Letter *

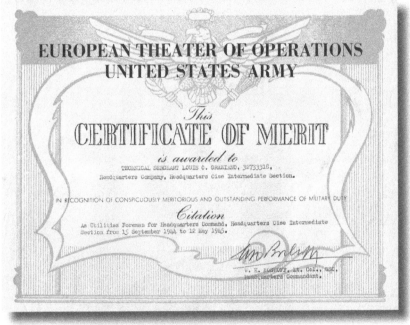

*Utilities Foreman Certificate of Merit ***

While I was in England, I went on leave for one week to Scotland. It was a beautiful country. I was able to see the changing of the guard at Edinburgh Castle while I was there. That was a sight to see!

It is a tradition to spit on one spot of the sidewalk as you walked by the castle, which I did. I even had my picture taken in kilts like the Scottish men wore.

*Louis in kilts ***
I tell everyone that I have "Betty Grable" legs.

Then I went back to my camp in England. The next day, the lieutenant, another soldier, and I had to go to town. I said to the lieutenant, "I know a shortcut to get there!" On our way, there were two American planes that hit head-on, a Spitfire and a Lancaster. We saw the crash when the planes hit the ground. The bodies were in pieces. I saw eyes looking at me; their arms and legs and all parts of their bodies were laying there. I said, "Lord, have mercy on their souls." I reported it, and they came and cleaned up the area. Then we went on into town and had lunch. My two men couldn't eat. I ate just a little. Then we went back to camp. I can still see the faces of those soldiers looking at me.

Crash site
*Louis at crash site ***

Louis, standing by the site of a crash between a Lancaster and a Spitfire

Before the invasion of France started, I was in England for about eighteen months. I was being trained to take a machine gun apart blindfolded and put it back together, in case it jammed in the darkness of night. After my training, I was busy getting my men trained on machine guns, pistols, rifles, and grenades, to get them ready to go to the ships to cross the English Channel. I had two soldiers who were conscientious objectors and would not carry a gun.

The next day, I took one of the big guns apart to clean it. After I had it apart, we had an air raid. General Thrasher came up and said, "Get that gun together!" I started to put it together in a hurry, but the last pin would not go in. The general said, "Give it to me, and I will do it." So, I gave it to him, and he couldn't do it either. I said, "Give it back to me, and I'll do it!" The pin went right in, and the general left.

The next day, I was trained on how to put fuses in the big shells that were used for the big guns. If you put a fuse in the front of it too far, you'd blow yourself up. They showed me one time, and by paying attention, I managed to do it right. I was a quick learner. I didn't want to be blown up, so I was really paying attention. We had to do hundreds of them, so I trained two of my men to help me. They did a good job.

3

PREPARING FOR D-DAY

Our next assignment was to travel seven hundred miles through England to our ships to cross the English Channel for the invasion of Omaha Beach.

*Trucks ready to be loaded ***
Our trucks lined up to go to the English Channel

We were supposed to have an assistant driver, but my assistant, Charlie Milazzo from Los Angeles, did not drive. I knew that, but I didn't say anything about it. We were good buddies, and he was good to have around. He kept me awake.

On this seven-hundred-mile journey, we were supposed to stop every one hundred miles for a ten-minute break. We had to keep a distance of two truck lengths apart. We drove straight through, and when we arrived the next day, we were to start loading the trucks onto the ships. I drove my tanker truck full of gasoline onto my ship. It took about three days before all the ships were loaded. My men and I boarded the LST (landing ship tank) to cross the English Channel.

Trucks Loaded *
The LST carrying the troops and equipment.

Before the invasion, Eisenhower's advisors told him his plan would be a suicide mission, so Eisenhower had a choice to make. They said if he stuck with his plan, he would be sending more than thirteen thousand men to their deaths. But if he didn't send the paratroopers in and the Germans were able to get reinforcements to the beaches, 156,000 men storming the beaches would become sitting ducks. After agonizing over this decision for three days, General Eisenhower decided to let the order stand. He would send in those paratroopers and pray his advisors were wrong. The paratroopers succeeded in cutting off German supply lines, setting the stage for a pivoted victory against Hitler's Nazi regime.

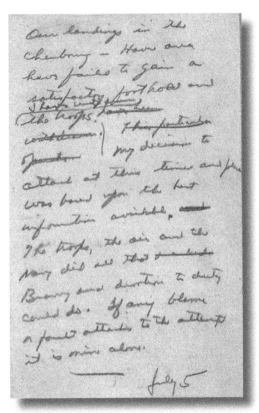

Eisenhower's handwritten draft *
Original note from Eisenhower

(Sent to me from General Eisenhower's granddaughter, Mary Jean Eisenhower, for me to share with others)

~~CONFIDENTIAL~~

Soldiers, Sailors and Airmen of the Allied Expeditionary Forces! You are about to embark upon the great Crusade, toward which we have striven these many months. ~~By it, we shall bring about,~~ In company with our brave Allies and brothers-in-arms on other Fronts, the destruction of the German war machine, the overthrow of Nazi tyranny, and the liberation of ~~the~~ oppressed peoples of Europe, and security for ourselves in a free world.

Your task will not be an easy one. Your enemy is well trained, well equipped and battle-hardened. ~~You may expect him to~~ fight savagely.

But this is the year 1944! Much has happened since the Nazi triumphs of 1940-41. The United Nations ~~We and our Allies~~ have inflicted upon the Germans great defeats, in open battle, man-to-man. ~~We shall do it again.~~ Our air offensive has seriously reduced their strength in the air and their capacity to wage war on the ground. Our Home Fronts have given us an overwhelming superiority in weapons and munitions of war, and placed at our disposal great reserves of trained fighting men. The tide has turned! The free men of the world are marching together to Victory!

The eyes of the world are upon you. The hopes and prayers of liberty-loving people everywhere march with you. ~~You will not fail them.~~

I have full confidence in your courage, devotion to duty and skill in battle. We ~~can, and we will win.~~

Good Luck! And ~~may~~ the blessing of Almighty God ~~rest~~ upon ~~you~~ this great and noble undertaking.

~~CONFIDENTIAL~~

Eisenhower's typed letter with corrections *

SUPREME HEADQUARTERS
ALLIED EXPEDITIONARY FORCE

Soldiers, Sailors and Airmen of the Allied Expeditionary Force!

You are about to embark upon the Great Crusade, toward which we have striven these many months. The eyes of the world are upon you. The hopes and prayers of liberty-loving people everywhere march with you. In company with our brave Allies and brothers-in-arms on other Fronts, you will bring about the destruction of the German war machine, the elimination of Nazi tyranny over the oppressed peoples of Europe, and security for ourselves in a free world.

Your task will not be an easy one. Your enemy is well trained, well equipped and battle-hardened. He will fight savagely.

But this is the year 1944 ! Much has happened since the Nazi triumphs of 1940-41. The United Nations have inflicted upon the Germans great defeats, in open battle, man-to-man. Our air offensive has seriously reduced their strength in the air and their capacity to wage war on the ground. Our Home Fronts have given us an overwhelming superiority in weapons and munitions of war, and placed at our disposal great reserves of trained fighting men. The tide has turned ! The free men of the world are marching together to Victory !

I have full confidence in your courage, devotion to duty and skill in battle. We will accept nothing less than full Victory !

Good Luck ! And let us all beseech the blessing of Almighty God upon this great and noble undertaking.

Dwight D Eisenhower

Each soldier, sailor, and airman received a copy of General Dwight D. Eisenhower's Order of the Day (**ABOVE**).

EISENHOWER
FOUNDATION
EisenhowerFoundation.net

Eisenhower's Final Order of the Day *

Final copy of Eisenhower's Order of the Day, which each soldier, sailor, and airman received from him. This was sent to me by Mary Jean Eisenhower.

Eisenhower talking to the soldiers

Here is a picture of General Dwight D. Eisenhower giving the 101st Airborne Division the order of the day. It is written that he had tears in his eyes while doing this. Eisenhower told his troops, "We will accept nothing less than full victory." This was hours before the planned invasion of Normandy, France.

Clickers Front *   *Clickers Back* *

Clickers like this played an important part in the liberation of France on June 6, 1944. Issued to the 101st Airborne Division, they enabled Allied troops to communicate without arousing the Germans. I purchased these at the WWII Memorial in Washington, DC.

Paratroopers

American airborne troops awaiting orders to jump. These troops were the first of the Allied invasion of Normandy on June 6, 1944.

The paratroopers were given the most dangerous mission of the entire invasion. They were to be dropped behind enemy lines to secure the roads and bridges and prevent German reinforcements from arriving once the invasion began— basically a suicide mission.

Shortly before they boarded their planes, their commander, Lieutenant Colonel Wolverton, gathered the paratroopers together and offered this prayer:

"God Almighty,
In a few short hours, we will be in battle with
the enemy. We do not join the battle afraid.
We do not ask favors or indulgences.
But, if You will, use us as Your instruments
for the Right and an aid in returning peace to the world.

We do not know or seek what our fate will be.
We only ask this ... that if die we must, that we die as
men would die ... without complaining, without pleading,
and safe in the feeling that we have done our best
for what we thought was right."

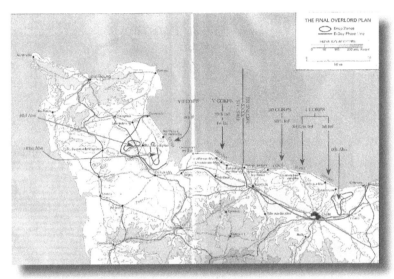

Overlord map
"Overlord"—the invasion plan for D-Day

"Overlord," the name of the plan for the most massive invasion ever, consisted of five assault phases: the beaches at Omaha, Juno, Utah, Gold, and Sword. Omaha Beach, a code name for one of the beaches in Normandy, France, was selected early in the Overlord planning since, at the time, it was undefended. On the negative side, the bluffs along the beach formed a significant tactical obstacle and were well suited for defense. Even after Field Marshal Erwin Rommel of the German army began fortifying the beach in autumn of 1943, it remained an attractive option because it offered a deep-water anchorage.

It was only three-quarters of a mile from all parts of the beach, with a full thirty-six feet of water at low tide, making it an ideal location for an artificial harbor for follow-on operations. The terrain behind the beach was much more suitable for motor transport than the neighboring Utah Beach. In February 1944, First US Army conducted a study of Omaha Beach, which concluded that, if defended by an infantry regiment, the configuration of the beach would multiply the combat power of the German troops and present a formidable defensive position assault, which would likely result in heavy casualties. If it was defended by a full infantry division, it would be impregnable. The US Army, right up to the time of the landing, thought that the beach was only defended by a single, understrength, poor-quality regiment. This would prove to be the most significant mistake in the US plan. The German forces on Omaha Beach were more than three times those anticipated. That is why I think we had so many more casualties than predicted.

My game face *
I am pictured on the right of the picture, with my "game face" on!
We were on our way to Omaha Beach.

The sea was rough, and we bounced around a lot. Some of the boys got seasick, but I didn't. When we got to Omaha Beach on June 6, 1944, we stayed back until it was our turn to go in. We were the third wave of the landings on the five assault beaches in Normandy on D-Day. Omaha Beach was the only one ever in doubt.

4

THE INVASION BEGINS—D-DAY

Card of Roosevelt's Prayer

Almighty God: Our sons, pride of our Nation, this day have set upon a mighty endeavor, a struggle to preserve our Republic, our religion, and our civilization, and to set free a suffering humanity.

Lead them straight and true; give strength to their arms, stoutness to their hearts, steadfastness in their faith.

They will need Thy blessings. Their road will be long and hard. For the enemy is strong. He may hurl back our forces. Success may not come with rushing speed, but we shall return again and again; and we know that by Thy grace, and by the righteousness of our cause, our sons will triumph.

They will be sore tried, by night and by day, without rest-until the victory is won. The darkness will be rent by noise and flame. Men's souls will be shaken with the violences of war.

For these men are lately drawn from the ways of peace. They fight not for the lust of conquest. They fight to end conquest. They fight to liberate. They fight to let justice arise, and tolerance and good will among all Thy people. They yearn but for the end of battle, for their return to the haven of home.

Some will never return. Embrace these, Father, and receive them, Thy heroic servants, into Thy kingdom.

And for us at home - fathers, mothers, children, wives, sisters, and brothers of brave men overseas - whose thoughts and prayers are ever with them - help us, Almighty God, to rededicate ourselves in renewed faith in Thee in this hour of great sacrifice.

Many people have urged that I call the Nation into a single day of special prayer. But because the road is long and the desire is great, I ask that our people devote themselves in a continuance of prayer. As we rise to each new day, and again when each day is spent, let words of prayer be on our lips, invoking Thy help to our efforts.

Give us strength, too - strength in our daily tasks, to redouble the contributions we make in the physical and the material support of our armed forces.

And let our hearts be stout, to wait out the long travail, to bear sorrows that may come, to impart our courage unto our sons wheresoever they may be.

And, O Lord, give us Faith. Give us Faith in Thee; Faith in our sons; Faith in each other; Faith in our united crusade. Let not the keenness of our spirit ever be dulled. Let not the impacts of temporary events, of temporal matters of but fleeting moment let not these deter us in our unconquerable purpose.

With Thy blessing, we shall prevail over the unholy forces of our enemy. Help us to conquer the apostles of greed and racial arrogancies. Lead us to the saving of our country, and with our sister Nations into a world unity that will spell a sure peace a peace invulnerable to the schemings of unworthy men. And a peace that will let all of men live in freedom, reaping the just rewards of their honest toil.

Thy will be done, Almighty God. Amen.

Roosevelt's Prayer

The First Wave

Within moments of landing, one-third of the assault troops of the first wave were casualties, even though the army superiors explained the invasion as if "all we had to do was walk up the beach." The assault was much more difficult than that. The infantrymen were told that the beach would have heavy hit from US aircraft, leaving holes in the sand to take as shelter; however, that was not the case. The beach was as flat as a smooth floor. The men said, "I think the army used us as cannon fodder."

You can imagine the horror we felt when we finally saw the beach, and it was completely flat—no craters and no cover. Of the forty soldiers of the first wave who went in on the landing craft, twelve survived that night.

We later learned that when they landed, they were hit at the same time as some of the boats to the left and right of us. We didn't know what to think. We just hoped and prayed it would be better for us. The most powerful weapons used by the Germans on Omaha Beach were two 88-mm PAKs. They were finally put out of commission.

The engineers' special brigades were marking lanes with white tape for troops, so they would not walk on a mine. We also used the white tape as a guide for us to drive our vehicles off the LST onto the shore. The brigadier general and the infantry commander landed with the second assault wave. He said, "Don't die on the beach, die up on the bluff, if you have to die, but get off the beaches, or you're sure to die!"

Then Came the Second Wave

The assault troops from First Battalion, Sixteenth Infantry, huddled inside their LCVP as they approached Omaha Beach around 0730 hours. During the second wave of landings, the tide had receded to reveal where Hitler had ordered the coasts of France to be fortified with miles of barbed wire, landmines, and machine gun bunkers. Some of the beach obstructions, tanks placed by the Germans, were exposed. This provided protection for some of the troops. The troops on the craft ahead had already disembarked and were wading to the shore.

Soldiers in water

Landing of Our Troops

As the second wave came up close to shore, Omaha Beach was so jammed with ships that troops couldn't get off—there was no place for the boats to come in. They began to circle out in the water. They stayed out there, some of them for two hours, just rocking and chasing around in a circle. They had to keep moving; otherwise, they would have made themselves too attractive as targets. It was terrible.

Besides having to fight the enemy on D-Day, one of the greatest enemies was seasickness. One of the troubles, and it was terrible, was that they transferred the men to small boats much farther out in the channel than they should have. The small boats were tossed about on the waves, which contributed to the seasickness of so many. Some of the men took so much Dramamine that they got sleepy.

Then Came the Third Wave, Which I Was Part Of

We pulled up as close as we could to the beach, with the LST loaded with vehicles. I drove a tanker truck full of gasoline onto the beach. I got out of it as soon as possible, getting all my weapons out with me, and laid down on the beach with the dead soldiers. I knew if that gasoline truck was hit, I would have been blown up. Every time after the Germans shot their guns, I would move a little closer to the cliff for protection. Then I got one man to shoot the flamethrower with me, as it takes two to handle it. I shot up the cliff and set the woods on fire. It was right under where the machine gun was, so that put that gun out of commission.

I then shot a flare up in the sky and over the cliff, so the navy would know where to fire. They saw what I wanted and did a good job for us. It helped us. I had thirty-five men but sadly lost two of them.

Navy Ships *

Navy ships were bombing the Germans to help us get ashore.

The next day, I told my men, "All of you who don't have guns, get one from the dead soldiers and follow me up the cliff." Most of my men did not have a gun, because they lost them in the water when they were trying to come ashore. The US Navy had collapsed a large slab of rocks, creating a mound of dirt about forty feet high, which gave protection while we were climbing up the cliff, which was about 100 to 170 feet high.

The Rangers were the first group of soldiers to climb the cliff. They were soaking wet, covered in mud, and under constant fire from the enemy. As they climbed the jagged cliff, they were sitting ducks. Their motto was "Rangers lead the way." As the Rangers reached the top, they broke up into smaller teams to take out the German stronghold and find the giant cannons they were sent to destroy. The first Ranger climbed the hundred-foot cliff in just ninety seconds.

Rangers climbing
Our brave Rangers

Shortly after reaching the top, two of the Rangers found the guns hidden in some bushes and used thermite grenades to destroy them, but their mission was far from over. Pointe du Hoc was a strategic vantage point. It was the highest cliff overlooking the English Channel on the coast of Normandy in northern France. During World War II, it was the highest point between Utah Beach to the west and Omaha Beach to the east. The Rangers had to hold ground at any cost.

Over the next two days, the Rangers endured wave after wave of German counterattacks. They were pinned between the German army and the cliffs they had just climbed. When help finally arrived two days after D-Day, less than 75 of the original 225 rangers were still in fighting condition. They had lost 70 percent of their men. But their tremendous sacrifice saved thousands of lives on the bloody sand of Omaha and Utah beaches. Without their heroic actions, it's possible our soldiers would have been driven back into the sea by the Germans.

After the Rangers climbed the cliff, we followed. But the Germans still had a lot of machine guns. We had to take them out one at a time. While we were going up the cliff, we saw a building up on one side. I saw someone moving and started to fire at that person; I realized it was a lady when I saw her skirt from the corner of the building. I didn't shoot and was glad, because I would have shot to kill. I didn't know what she was doing there, but I kept on climbing.

The lady was coming around the corner of the building at the top left of this picture.

Top of cliff building*
The building that was on one side of the cliff.

The night before we hit the beach, we had a prayer meeting, and that was one night *everyone* prayed. I was twenty-one when I hit Omaha Beach. We were trained to kill or be killed. The machine gun could fire 350 rounds a minute. The assignment was one of the most dangerous on the battlefield. The machine gun teams were prime targets for the German snipers, because they could not move easily once in place.

The assault beach zones repeatedly uncovered new enemy positions along the hedgerows farther to the east. Some artillery had been brought ashore, and we tried to get its support. But the angle presented by the bluff overlooking the beach made it impossible at this range. So, the bitter struggle went on for one-gun position after another. Although we didn't realize it yet, the major responsibility for securing and holding a beachhead in the Twenty-Ninth Division sector of Omaha Beach was on our shoulders.

Disaster came pouring from every direction at GIs who survived the brutal landings to get ashore. The GIs were stunned as they saw their buddies go down, get shot, or get blown into pieces. The remaining men who had amazingly survived were somehow able to continue fighting. We were losing so many soldiers, General Omar Bradley thought Omaha was lost and suspended sending reinforcements. But the Rangers persevered and took Pointe du Hoc. While many were dying on the beach, many brave men were still fighting. A German general was wounded, which turned the tide. This caused wounded and shell-shocked GIs to rally and attack the bluff's defenses.

Soldiers were still being killed on the beaches. A wounded

soldier was heard yelling, "Don't surrender!" So, we kept on fighting, and we got the best of them. That was a terrible night. We finally got help for the wounded soldiers. We took to the motto, "Let us go inland and be killed." Omaha Beach is now a historic tale of victory where soldiers denied defeat. And then ...

The Fourth Wave Came up the Beach

The fourth wave came up with more trucks. The first, second, and third waves had it rough. The Germans quickly brought up replacements. Our B Company encountered heavy machine gun and sniper fire, while advancing onto St. Laurent-Vierville. The E Company met severe resistance trying to move south around the town. Our lieutenant died bravely in that attempt.

We captured twenty-three of the commandos, and eighteen were executed by the Americans for contravening the rules of war by wearing enemy uniforms.

We had lost 85 percent of our soldiers from the first wave and also some from the second, third, and fourth waves during the invasion when we hit Omaha Beach. The difficulties encountered on "Bloody Omaha" were due to the more difficult terrain on this coastline, the unexpected presence of a first-rate German division at the beach, and inadequate fire support. Yet, despite all of these problems, by the end of D-day, the Atlantic wall had been breached, and the US Army Corps were firmly entrenched on the French coast. There were more than ten times as many casualties on Omaha Beach than there were on the other beaches, which were incredibly hard fought as well.

Omaha Beach was almost four miles long. One innovation for the Normandy landing was the use of rocket craft. These LCT(R) (3) carried 1,080 five-inch rockets. A total of nine thousand rockets were fired in the opening bombardment from nine LCTs, but most accounts suggest their gunfire missed the beach, leaving no cover for the soldiers coming ashore. Some of the more unusual weapons at Omaha Beach were the remote-control "Goliath" demolition vehicles. These contained a high-explosive charge and were intended to attack tanks or landing craft. However, they arrived only a day before the landings, and it was recorded they were not used in combat.

Hitler's forces were battle-tested and hardened fighters, while most of the Allied troops had yet to see combat. The trouble was that this whole beach was full of obstacles. It was written that the Germans said, "The war will be won or lost on the beaches. We'll have only one chance to stop the enemy, and that's while he's in the water struggling to get ashore."

Field Marshal Erwin Rommel had planted the beach with every kind of miserable, vicious obstacle there was, and most of them were mined. Therefore, if we had tried to come in with vessels, we would have just been blown up or stabbed in the bottom and sunk. We had to have the low tide to see those obstacles.

Obstacles
Obstacles on the beach

Invasion D-Day

On June 6, 1944, more than 156,000 American, British, Canadian, and other Allied forces stormed the fortified beaches of France's Normandy. The invasion, dubbed "Operation Overlord," led by Dwight D. Eisenhower was the largest amphibious military assault in history. The invasion marked a significant victory and signaled the beginning of the end for Hitler's Third Reich.

The other thing was that the beach was very heavily fortified and well manned. For example, there were four batteries of artillery and eighty-five machine gun nests. Then there were all the concrete fortifications. There were eight big bunkers, each with a 75-mm gun and sometimes larger ones. Each gun had its local automatic weapons. There were eighteen mortar pits, thirty-five pill boxes, each with guns ranging from machine guns to 88-mm weapons. They had eighteen antitank guns—normally 88-mm—and about twenty rocket-launching sites.

Their bunkers were very solidly constructed and almost impossible to knock out. Each was like a sealed wall. You couldn't even reach the wall in most cases. In front of the wall was a concrete apron. Normally the bunkers were camouflaged with rock and other materials. Another thing that made Omaha tough was the 352nd German Division, which manned all these defenses and really held the beach.

Cliff with bunker *
German artillery gun on cliffs above Normandy Beach

The 352ⁿᵈ German Division was there waiting for us. Our intelligence advised us they moved up almost on the eve of the battle, but they were wrong. Information from the French resistance was very good. They told us a great deal. They got a lot of information into us, and when we gave them the word, they did some very effective work in blocking roads and blowing up facilities used by the Germans. They were very active. The greatest error we made in intelligence was about the German troops at Omaha. We were too late in getting the information about the 352nd defending Omaha Beach. We knew something about it at the very last minute, so we kept fighting and holding on until reinforcements came in and helped us.

5

My Journey Through France

Now we started fighting our way to Saint-Lô, France, a town about twenty miles from Omaha Beach. We made it through and arrived there on July 18, 1944. It took forty-three days to secure the city of Saint-Lô. Although the city was captured, task forces continued to receive severe enemy fire.

*Louis standing among ruins ***
Ruins on the way to Reims, France. (Arrow pointing to me)

Ruins #1*

Ruins #2*
More pictures of ruins on the road to Reims, France.

We kept on fighting our way until we got to Reims, where General Thrasher was put in charge of the city and set up his headquarters. He called me in to go and buy the things we needed to set up headquarters and for the troops who were going to stay there. He put me in charge of utilities, and I had a crew of thirty-five men. I had to go and buy some materials, so I took one man with me to the lumber yard. I had a little book that had English and French in it.

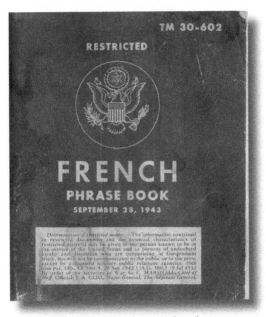

French translation book *
My personal French-English translation
book given to me in France

When I got to town, I pointed to the word of the things I wanted, but the merchant would not sell them to me. I went back to camp, got my .45 and four of my men, and we went back to get the materials. The merchant said no again, so I got my .45 out and told my men to load up the material. Then I gave him the paper for him to go and get his money from the army. I thought I was going to get in trouble, but I didn't. I think he was afraid to start trouble; he probably thought I would come back and get him. I knew he had what I needed, but he didn't want to sell it to the Americans. I looked at him and said, "I thought we are here to free your country, and you don't want to help us?" I went back to camp and told the general how I got the things we needed. He said, "We may hear from that," but we didn't.

I also had a crew of men who I assigned to different jobs around the city from an office in a building where Americans stayed. We had to use our plumbing and electrical skills for anything that had to be fixed. One day, Brigadier General Thrasher came up to me and said, "I need for you and one of your men to put a telephone in General Eisenhower's quarters." I took Buck with me. We couldn't tell anybody what we had to do. We had to run wire through the town and fields while at the same time looking out for mines. When we arrived there, we were there for two days before we went back. General Eisenhower was good to us while we were there. He was a man I respected and looked up to. It was an honor to serve under him.

When I got back to camp, I got word the German planes had bombed and stripped the supply depots. Clerks, typists, and truck drivers from Headquarters of OISE Section, France, had to be hastily pressed into service as anti-aircraft crews. Being unfamiliar with the fifty-caliber machine guns, they had to be trained quickly. Serving as instructors for the training were Sergeant Donald Steuwer of Eau Claire, Wisconsin, and me. We got them ready to help with the breakthrough of the Germans.

One night, we were being shot at by the Germans. My buddy Buck knocked me down to the ground, because he saw the Germans shooting toward me. He saved my life. I said, "You can knock me down anytime." I told my truck drivers to shoot those machine guns and help us. They said they were truck drivers and didn't know how to shoot. I said, "When they start shooting at you, you will learn in a hurry!" They did, and it helped us to overtake the Germans. Don't ever say you don't know how.

I had trained my buddy, Buck, on what had to be done in case something happened to me. It's a good thing I did, because during the time of the Battle of the Bulge, I was sent to Reims, France, with Headquarters OISE Intermediate Section Theater Service Forces, European Theater. The American soldiers were cut off for six weeks by the German soldiers. They had them surrounded, so Captain Wormhoudt came in one night to my quarters and asked me to go on a mission. I asked him if it was a request or an order, and he said, "I can make it an order." My reply to him was, "Let's go!" I felt like I had been in the worst possible battle of my life at Omaha Beach, so what could be worse?

The captain said we had to go and find a company of troops from the Third Army Division who were lost and needed to get to Bastogne, Belgium, to reinforce General George Patton's troops, who were cut off by the Germans. We found them somewhere between Reims, France, and Metz, France, and escorted them to Bastogne. Bastogne played a critical role in the Battle of the Bulge. The capture of Bastogne was the goal of the Battle of the Bulge. Bastogne provided a road junction in rough terrain where few roads existed; it would open a valuable pathway further north for German expansion. The Belgian town was defended by the US 101st Airborne Division, which had to be reinforced by troops who staggered in from other battlefields. Food, medical supplies, and other resources eroded as bad weather and relentless German assaults threatened the Americans' ability to hold out.

We were very worried about our supplies, not knowing if we were going to have enough food, ammunition, and warm clothes to last us until we got back to Reims, France. There were many prayers said at that time. Our food supply consisted of canned C-Rations, not an ideal meal, but it sustained us. Our ammunition lasted, but we did not have enough warm clothes to change into when ours got wet from all the snow.

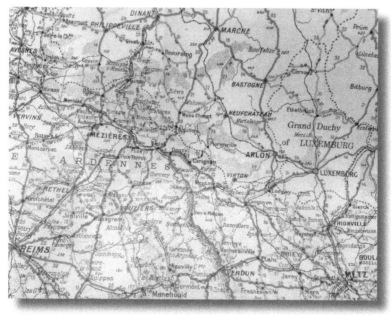

My map of France *

This is a map of France and Belgium that was given to me, so we could find our way. I just made a copy of the section, so you could note the distance between Reims, Metz, and Bastogne.

The closer we got to Bastogne, the more the attacks worsened. It was all we could do to stay alive. It was snowing hard, and you couldn't see where you were going. At Bastogne, the Americans were outnumbered five to one, but we held firm throughout the fighting. Some of our soldiers were wounded. One was calling for his father. I thought that was odd, because most called for their mothers. We, as young men, were having to grow up fast.

General Patton had a plan to break through the German lines and enter Bastogne, relieving the valiant soldiers and ultimately pushing the Germans across the Rhine River.

Eisenhower at Bastogne

The temperature was below zero, and I had not been issued combat boots. My feet froze during the Battle of the Bulge, but at that time, I didn't think about my feet. I just tried to stay alive. We did not have proper clothing or gear.

From Bastogne, the captain and I went back to Reims, France. I went to the dispensary, and they started to treat my feet. My feet were swollen, and there was fluid draining from the sores. I remember they also used hoops over them to keep the sheets from touching my feet. To this day, I still use a triangle pillow to keep the sheets off of my feet. If I had not gone to the dispensary when I did, amputation would have been the only option left. Trench feet was the term they were using if amputation was to take place.

My buddy Buck had done a good job. He was ready for me to be back! One night we had an air raid—German planes were overhead. When there was an air raid, the whole city had to be in blackout. I saw some buildings with lights on, and I told the major that I was going to drive around with two of my men and shoot them out. He said,

"You can't do that … but I don't know anything about it." I said, "Thank you." We then went around the city and shot them out. The French made a big deal about it, but nobody knew who did it. There were no lights on at the next air raid.

Then, about one month later, we had another air raid. In our camp we had a brick wall about eight feet high, and the enemy on the other side of the wall set a can of gasoline on fire to reveal our position. I had my men with their guns looking over the wall. I jumped over the wall and put out the fire. They had to throw a rope over the wall to help me get back over. We never had this problem again.

6

My Adventures in Reims, France

I was good to my men; some of them wanted a class-A pass, so they could stay out all night. They all knew they had to be back for reveille. One of the boys kept coming in late, so I told him to give me back his pass, and I might possibly take his CPL stripes too. He said, "Take your shirt off and come outside!" My men said, "You're not going out there, are you?" "Oh, yes, I am!" The boys knew I was a hairdresser at home, and they thought I would not have a chance, because he was bigger than me. I went out there and beat the hell out of him and didn't have any more trouble with him. They didn't know I boxed at home. Living next door to where they trained boxers, I used to get in and practice with them.

One night, two of my men were fighting—for what reason, I didn't know. I had all the troops' quarters wired up to my quarters, so I could keep track of them. I heard them fighting, and I got up and went to see what that was all about. One man had a knife, and he was just about to stab the other man when I got the knife from him. I took him into my quarters to stay the rest of the night. That gave them time to cool off.

The next morning, I had them shake hands. That took care of that problem.

I always tried to keep peace with all my men; they did listen to me, and I knew I had their respect and they would do anything for me. Being a master sergeant, I learned how to treat people. You treat them how you want to be treated. That was not the case with all master sergeants.

Another day, I was walking through the park when I saw two soldiers and a French cop. I looked at the French cop, and he looked at me. We both thought that the soldiers did not look like Americans, even though they were wearing American uniforms. He was the closest to them. I gave him the eye to get them. He grabbed one of the soldiers, and the soldier threw the cop to the ground. The other one got away. There were too many children in the park, so I didn't dare shoot at him. I jumped in to help the cop out and got the soldier by his arm and put it behind him. I could have broken if off. He kept saying "comrade," and I said, "If you say that one more time, I will put this .45 through you!" He did not say it again.

Headquarters was about eight blocks away, and I started walking him there. While I was walking him, the French people were spitting at him, and I was getting hit too. I was lucky—I saw my buddy coming. I stopped him and put the soldier in the back of the truck with my knee on his back, still holding his arm behind him. I got him to headquarters and took his shirt off, and he had "SS" on his arm, which meant he was a German suicide soldier. His wearing an American uniform meant he had to be executed by the Americans, according to contravening rules of war.

One night, one of the MPs on duty came to my quarters and asked me to ride around the city with him. I said okay, and we left. We saw an underground entrance, and he said, "Let's check it out!" I said okay, and he said, "You go first, and I will cover you!"

I said, "You are on duty; I will cover *you!*" We went in, and there were German soldiers in there. They heard us coming, set their order papers on fire, and got away. We found a ladder going up into our motor pool. I put a concrete slab over the entry and backed up a truck wheel over it. Then we waited about ten days.

We figured they might come back, so I took six soldiers with me and told them what was down there. We went in, and the Germans heard us and ran for the ladder. But they could not get out. There were four of them. We got them and took them to headquarters and turned them in.

In my job, I oversaw German prisoners at my camp. I would put them to work around the camp. One evening, when I was taking the flag down, the German prisoners would not stand at attention. They laid down on the ground. I told them they had better get up, but they didn't. The next day, I punished them and made them carry logs. Every time they came around, I would put another log on their arms until they couldn't walk anymore. I didn't have any more trouble with them when the flag came down.

One time I had one of the German soldiers keep the officers' club clean. A lot of our donuts were missing all the time. I caught him one day and made him stand outside in the hot sun and eat a big pan of donuts. I would not give him any water. I didn't have any donuts missing anymore. I took care of that problem along with many other problems.

One day I was working with Major Campbell, the engineer in charge of the city of Reims, France. The general came up and asked the major to take the German prefab houses and build a large mess hall to be able to feed all the troops. The major tried for about three weeks and still could not figure it out. One day we were out there, and the general came up and asked the major, "What is your problem? You have nothing done!" The general looked at me and asked me if I could get them up. I said, "Yes, I can, General. If you and I can step to the side, I will tell you what I want." He said okay and he told the major to stay right there. I said to the general, "If you let me use the German prisoners and guards who speak German and English, I will build your mess hall."

He quickly said, "You got it!"

German Prisoners *
These were the German prisoners I used
to help me build the mess hall.

The general left, and the major said, "You are not an engineer. How do you think you are going to do it?" I wouldn't tell him how I was going to do it. Within three weeks, I had completed the mess hall. The German prisoners knew what to do, according to my instructions about the prefabs. You don't have to be an engineer; you must use your head. The next thing the general did was transfer the major out and put me in charge of the city of Reims, France. I oversaw all the buildings that American soldiers used and occupied and the headquarters offices.

After successfully getting the mess hall built, General Thrasher approached me about building an open-air theater for the troops in Reims. So, my men and I built the Headquarters Command US Army Amphitheater, also called the Municipal Theater. It was a gigantic outdoor theater with two thousand seats, which became one of the most popular entertainment centers in Reims. As I was working on the building with my men, who should come up but General Thrasher, to see how it was coming. He said, "Do you know how to do the acoustics for the sound?"

I said, "Yes, sir." When he left, I said to myself, "What in the hell is acoustics?" I went and got a book to learn how to do it. Don't ever say you don't know how to do something; there is always a way. Just read the book! I got the building built and then tackled the acoustics. I was proud of myself for doing a good job with that.

My handbook *
*This is the handbook given to me at
headquarters in Reims, France.*

Jane Froman
This picture was taken from the Froman, Jane (1907–
1980), Papers, 1891–1980 (C3695) Manuscript Collection.
The State Historical Society of Missouri, Photograph
Collection.Photo by the US Army Signal Corps.

Jane Froman was the first star to sing in the amphitheater I built with my men. She had been in a plane crash and was on crutches. The pilot had saved her life. I helped her to the stage, and she held on to the microphone. I took her crutches and went to the sound room to take care of the sound. She was a great singer, and the troops enjoyed her. Later that day, her husband came into my office. I enjoyed talking to him.

Another interesting thing happened when I was building the theater. I had to dig down to put the building up, because the seats had to be up, to be able to look down on the stage. While we were digging, we hit a block wall. The boys said,

"Let's break a hole and see what is in there." We found a Frenchman's wine cellar! We went in and got the bottles that had the most dust on them, because they were the oldest. The next day, the Frenchman went and reported it to the general. No one would say who had done it, so when payday came, the general took a few cents from all the troops in that company to reimburse the man. We had a good time drinking the champagne from the wine cellar.

While I was in France, I went on furlough and visited Switzerland. When we arrived in Switzerland, a hotel was having an opening celebration, so we joined in. Below are pictures from my visit.

Alps #1 *   *Alps #2 **

Louis, standing on the top of the second-highest Alpine peak in Switzerland, looking down on the cable car.

Louis & Charlie, Switzerland*
*Charles Milazzo and Louis in Switzerland. He
is the brother-in-law of actress Ida Lupino.*

Ida Lupino was an actress during WWII. One part she played in a movie was of a lieutenant with the Women's Ambulance and Defense Corps of America. The rank wasn't official, but the urge to serve was genuine. Private organizations like the corps sprang up in response to American women's desire to contribute to the nation's defense.

"The Little Red Schoolhouse"

Among the several buildings in Reims, I took care of this building known as "the Little Red Schoolhouse." This was where the women lived and where the Instrument of Surrender was signed. It was also headquarters for General Eisenhower. I had to keep everything running and in good shape. Some buildings were where the troops lived, some served as offices, and one was a big mess hall where the troops ate. My buddy Buck's girlfriend, Jen, was the mess sergeant.

I got Buck promoted to staff sergeant, and one day after supper, Buck said, "We ought to go and see the ladies play ball." So, Buck, Jen, and I went to the ball game, and we watched them play.

I asked Jen, "Who is that girl?"

She said, "Her name is Bobbie, and she is my best friend!" Bobbie was the name she went by, because she did not want to be called by her real name, "Eula" Estelle Shaneyfelt.

The next day, I went into the orderly room, where I knew

she worked. A girl who worked in the same office asked me what I wanted, and I said, "I am here to see Bobbie." She said she would go and get her for me. Bobbie came out, and we talked. I asked her for a date the next night, and she said okay. I went the next night to get her, and the girls told me she had already left with someone else. When she returned, the girls told her she would not get another chance, but she said, "Yes, I will!"

After a couple of weeks, I went and asked her again for another date, and she said yes. I went to pick her up, and she was there this time! Buck, Jen, Bobbie, and I went out. After that night, the four of us went out all the time. We were quite a foursome, always together. One night, we were walking back to camp from one of the clubs. When we were about two blocks from camp, I saw there was a man behind us. I kept looking out of the corner of my eye, and all at once he started to grab Bobbie by the neck. I turned around and knocked him down and told them to go back to camp. Then I beat the hell out of him. I left him lying there, and I went back to camp. I was quite a fighter in my younger days.

One night when we all went out to a nightclub in Reims, we started drinking champagne. When we left the nightclub, we saw an old Catholic church and decided to explore it. The doors were unlocked, so we entered this beautiful church. There was a winding staircase in it, and we all started our journey up the stairs, not feeling too much pain. After winding around and around the staircase, we were not feeling so well. Coming down was a problem also.

The next morning, when Bobbie went in to work, her captain asked her what was wrong. She looked pale and sick.

After Bobbie told her about our night's excursion, she kidded her all day long.

One night, Buck, Jen, Bobbie, and I went out, and as we were coming back to camp, we decided to go to the kitchen and cook ourselves a steak. No one should be in the kitchen after hours. Who should come in and catch us but Lieutenant Colonel W. H. Boshoff! He said, "What are you all doing here?"

I jumped up and said, "Colonel, how do you like your steak?" So, that took care of that. You see, use your head!

Col. Bushoff, Jen, Buck *

Things were getting serious with Bobbie, and I sent home for an engagement ring to give to her. One night, we went to the officers' club for a dance, and I realized that this was "the night." After a few dances, we went to the bar to have a drink. She turned around, and I offered her the ring. This was in June 1945. She said yes. I was very happy, because I truly loved her.

*My Proposal ***
My proposal to Bobbie was in the officers' club called The Utilities "Dug Out" Club, otherwise known as "Boshoff's Pub." I built it with the help of my men from lumber taken from an old barn we took down. It came out well, especially with the long bar we built.

Bobbie and I were married on October 2, 1945. We wore our uniforms at our wedding. Buck and Jen stood up with us. We got married at the courthouse in Reims, France. Colonel Boshoff lent me his car, so I could take my beautiful wife to Paris for our honeymoon. This was only possible because Paris had been freed on August 25, 1945. We stayed a week, but we were unable to live together until we got back to the

States. We got married by a priest when we got discharged and arrived back in New York.

Club Invitation *

This is a copy of the invitation to the official opening of our club.

Double Exposure Picture *↑
Arrow points to me and Bobbie.

Some of the officers who enjoyed the officers' club in Reims along with me and my beautiful wife.

Band *
Some of the army boys who provided
our music in the officers' club.

Group around table *
Some of the officers enjoying some down
time Buck is first on the left)

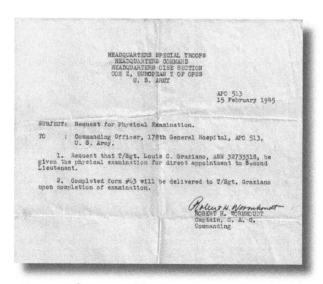

Request for second lieutenant appointment*

This was a request for a physical, put in by Robert

Wormhoudt, which would enable me to be appointed a second lieutenant.

The request for a physical resulted because of a letter written to my colonel from my captain. Below is an excerpt from that letter.

> *I have observed Sergeant Graziano's soldierly manner, attention to duty and sincere loyalty to a cause. During the past two months, Sergeant Graziano has worked directly under me as Foreman of the Utilities Center. Without his assistance as Foreman there is doubt as to whether we could have accomplished our work with such expediency.*
>
> *Sergeant Graziano possesses the rare quality of starting a job and finishing it- thoroughly. He does not need to be told, how, when, or why - he gets results. He is a born gentleman and at all times exemplifies this quality. He knows how to deal with men and by this manner has gotten the most out of them and too - their respect. He is most courteous at all times. He possesses leadership. Sergeant Graziano possesses, in addition to these qualities, a resourcefulness necessary to the service. His inventiveness has surmounted many problems which in the beginning seemed impossible. In this connection his ability is invaluable.*

It has been necessary during this period to work both night and day. Never has he thought of himself selfishly. He has always volunteered for any duty in most instances has carried our work far into the night. He could have delegated this work to others. His loyalty to duty has forbade this. His willingness prevailed in all endeavors.

It is hoped that Sergeant Graziano has the opportunity to serve his country in a grade commensurate with his abilities and understanding. Were he given this opportunity, the service will have gained an officer well equipped to do any or all tasks given.

I, therefore recommend, Sergeant Graziano be commissioned an officer in the Army of the United States.

I was grateful and honored by this offer to commission me an officer in the US Army and also for the wonderful things he had to say about my work. However, if I had accepted the position, I would have had to stay in the army longer, and I knew I was ready to go home. So, with much deliberation over this, I declined the promotion.

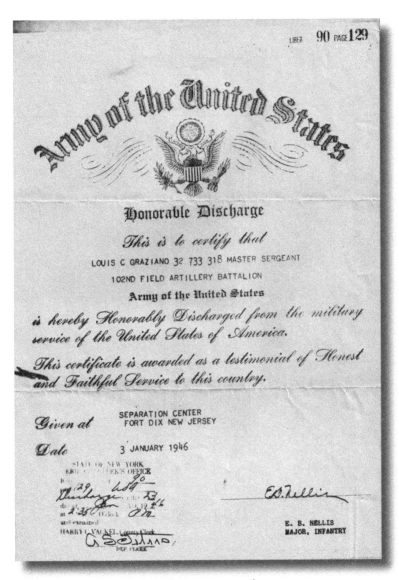

Discharge papers*

7

THE END OF THE WAR—GERMANY AND JAPAN SURRENDER

Germans signing in war room

The war ended with the signing of the Instrument of Surrender on May 7, 1945 between the German High Command and Walter Bedell Smith, chief of staff of SHAEF (Supreme

Headquarters Allied Expeditionary Force), on behalf of Dwight D. Eisenhower. The signing took place at the Little Red Schoolhouse in Reims, France, which was being used as Supreme Headquarters of the Allied Expeditionary Force, where General Eisenhower and his staff were quartered. I was present for the signing of the surrender. I was honored to be in that room that day.

Victory Order of the Day *

The atomic bomb was dropped August 6, 1945 on Hiroshima, Japan. It is documented that there was no enemy opposition to the plane carrying the atomic bomb. It was flying at thirty thousand feet. The Japanese had no defense against high-flying airplanes. The plane was just coming out of the turn when the bomb exploded. It took forty-three seconds from the time the bomb left the plane until it exploded. The entire city of Hiroshima was covered with black smoke and dust. The bomb exploded 1,800 feet above the ground, so the shockwave came down and out over the city.

Atomic Bomb

President Harry S. Truman implored the Japanese to surrender after the bomb was dropped, to avoid more destruction.

Truman
President Truman announces the surrender of Japan—and the impending end of World War II, August 14,1945

Below are pictures of the Japanese surrender on September 2, 1945.

Japanese coming to sign

Emperor Hirohito (top hat) at the Japanese surrender with General MacArthur

MacArthur Signing

Japan's Instrument of Surrender

A copy of the Instrument of Surrender with the Japanese sent to me

Victory Parade *

This is a picture of the Victory Parade when the war ended. I am in the honor guard row, the fourth from the left, next to the flag. My men are the first group of soldiers you see marching. My wife, Bobbie, is with the women behind me.

Paris Celebration

American servicemen in Paris celebrating after receiving news that the emperor of Japan had surrendered.

The Famous Kiss

Famous Kiss

People were celebrating moments after news broke that Japan had surrendered, bringing an end to WW II. The sailor and the nurse kissed in their excitement. They both showed the elation of two people whose lives were scarred by war who would now look forward to peace.

He had remembered the kindness and dedication shown by American nurses when they were taking care of all the wounded soldiers. The nurse was a dental hygienist and was a native of Austria, who had lost her parents to the Holocaust.

The picture was taken in Times Square in New York City on August 14, 1945.

8

BOBBIE'S RESCUE AND OUR RETURN HOME

At the end of the war, on December 14, 1945, the WAACs (Women's Army Auxiliary Corps, later WACs, Women's Army Corps) boarded the *Athos II* to return home. Little did they know the trouble they would endure.

The *Athos II* left Le Havre, France, on December 14, 1945, bound for New York. They did not have any fuel at Le Havre, so the ship had to cross the channel to get fuel. After fueling the ship, it pulled out of Southampton, England, on December 15 and was expected to arrive in New York on December 25. So much for Christmas that year! It would have been a great Christmas present for Bobbie to get home on the twenty-fifth. That did not happen. The ship ran into a terrific storm on December 21. The passengers said the French captain gave up the ship for lost. They had to pull into the Azores Islands. This was the worst storm the Atlantic had seen in the past twenty-five years.

WAAC Major Katherine L. St. John, a native of Frankfort, Kentucky, was the senior officer in charge of the WAACs.

She formerly served as staff director of WAACs assigned to the Ninth Air Force. The storm hit on December 21 at 1:30 p.m., while they were having their date hour in the officers' lounge. The date hour was a four-hour period held each day for WAACs and army enlisted personnel.

Soldiers and WAACs and furniture were thrown all over the place. There was no hysteria at all when the WAACs were ordered below as ballast, even though one girl fainted and one suffered a broken bone. Another had all her front teeth knocked out. Orange juice and eggs and mashed potatoes were all over the place, and much of their food was ruined.

The USS *Enterprise* came to the Azores Islands to rescue the ladies. The *Enterprise* carried fifteen stretchers and eighteen walking patients along with the others from the *Athos II* and the USS *Hood,* another ship they used to transport soldiers home. It took the WAACs about thirty days to reach the United States because of the storm and having to wait for the *Enterprise* to come to their rescue. The WAACs were the darlings of the *Enterprise,* not only because it was the first time the ship had carried females as passengers, but also because of their bravery aboard the *Athos II.* Officers said the USS *Enterprise* would no longer be used as a troop ship but would be laid up to become a shrine for American naval power in this war.

The three pictures below were all in a booklet given to my wife as she boarded the *Enterprise.*

Front of welcome booklet *
Welcome booklet given to my wife, Bobbie,
when she boarded the Enterprise.

The next two pages were one of the inside pages and the back of the booklet.

Facts and Figures of the "Big E"

Following are facts and figures on the war, record, size, and certain characteristics of the "Big E":

Planes shot down	911	Length of Hanger Deck	548 feet
Ships sunk	71	Beam at waterline	104 feet
Ships damaged and probably sunk	192	Height of uppermost antenna	About 158 feet above waterline
Plane landings	Over 45,000	Height of flight deck	About 60 feet above waterline
Planes carried aboard	More than 80 fighters, dive bombers and torpedo planes	Height of hanger deck	About 28 feet above waterline
Anti-aircraft armament	5 inch, 40MM, and 20MM	Average draft	About 28 feet
Battle complement	Over 2500	Horsepower	120,000
Present reduced complement	About 1250	Propellers	4
Displacement	Approximately 30,000 tons	Boilers	9
Overall length	827 feet, 4 inches	Distance travelled since commissioning	Over 412,000 miles
Length of Flight Deck	814 feet		

Facts & Figures of the Big E*

The United States Ship Enterprise

Launched on 3 October 1936, the U. S. S. ENTER-PRISE (CV6) is the seventh United States naval vessel to bear that name. The first was a sloop captured from the British and commanded by General Benedict Arnold during the Revolutionary War. Most famous of the early ships was the "Lucky Little Enterprise", the third of that name. In commission from 1799 to 1823, she was commanded by such illustrious naval heroes as Stephen Decatur, David Porter and Isaac Hull. Her record was achieved mainly in action against France in 1799 and 1800, against the Barbary pirates, and in the War of 1812.

Upon her commissioning into active service on 12 May 1938, the present Enterprise became a part of the Atlantic Fleet. After a shake-down cruise to Rio de Janeiro and participation in the winter fleet maneuvers in the Caribbean Sea, she received orders to the Pacific Fleet.

On the morning of 7th December 1941, the Enterprise was less than 200 miles from Pearl Harbor returning there after delivering twelve fighter-planes to the Marine garrison on Wake Island. Planes launched from her flight deck that morning intercepted the enemy planes attacking Oahu.

In the following years of the Pacific War, the "Big E" took part in every major operation of that theater with the exception of the Battle of the Coral Sea. She received the last of the damaging fifteen direct hits and near misses that she sustained during the war on the morning of 14 May 1945 when a Japanese kamikaze plane crashed through the flight deck just aft of number one elevator. The force of the explosion blew the elevator over 400 feet in the air. The section of a wing on the port bulkhead in the forward part of the hanger deck was blown on to the hanger deck when a kamikaze attempting to hit the ship crashed into the sea near the port quarter on last 11th April.

The Enterprise is the only large carrier to hold the Presidential Unit Citation, and the only one to be awarded it for service in the Pacific area.

The US Ship Enterprise *

When the war ended, I headed home from Reims, France, on the USS *Liberty*.

I was very surprised to see my best friend, who went in the service the same day as I did, working on the ship. So, I had the run of the ship!

We encountered a terrible storm. It was so bad that if the ship had tilted two more degrees, it would have tipped over. It kept us from returning to Fort Dix, New Jersey, so we headed toward Norfolk, Virginia. We docked in Norfolk on Christmas Day. What a great Christmas present it was to be on US soil.

We all had to report to Fort Dix to get discharged. When we arrived in Norfolk, we were told that all the boys needing to go to New York might be delayed two weeks, because there was no one in charge to take them. I spoke to the officer and told him I was a master sergeant from New York and asked him to put me in charge, and I would get us all to Fort Dix.

He agreed with my wishes, and I made it happen. Again, use your head, and it pays off! We all got home sooner than we would have otherwise.

After I got discharged, I went home to East Aurora, New York, to my parents' house. It was a joyful reunion. My dad had to play the record for me that I had sent to him. I could see how proud he was of me and how thankful he was for my safe return home.

I asked him, "Did I really say all of those things on the record?"

He said, "Yes, and they all came true. You and the other soldiers did a good job."

I said, "Dad, we accomplished our mission."

My family had a big reunion to celebrate my return home. Everyone was asking about Bobbie. Because I married in France, my family thought my wife was a French girl. I had not told them she was from Alabama. I had been calling her sister to see if she had made it home. With us leaving on different ships on different days, I had no idea where she was. All I could do was pray for her safety. I never dreamed it would be a month later before I would see her.

Bobbie wrote me a letter while she was in the Azores Islands waiting for a ship to pick her and the other ladies up to transport them to the States.

Bobbie's Envelope *

The envelope Bobbie's letter was in. Please note the cost of an airmail stamp in 1946.

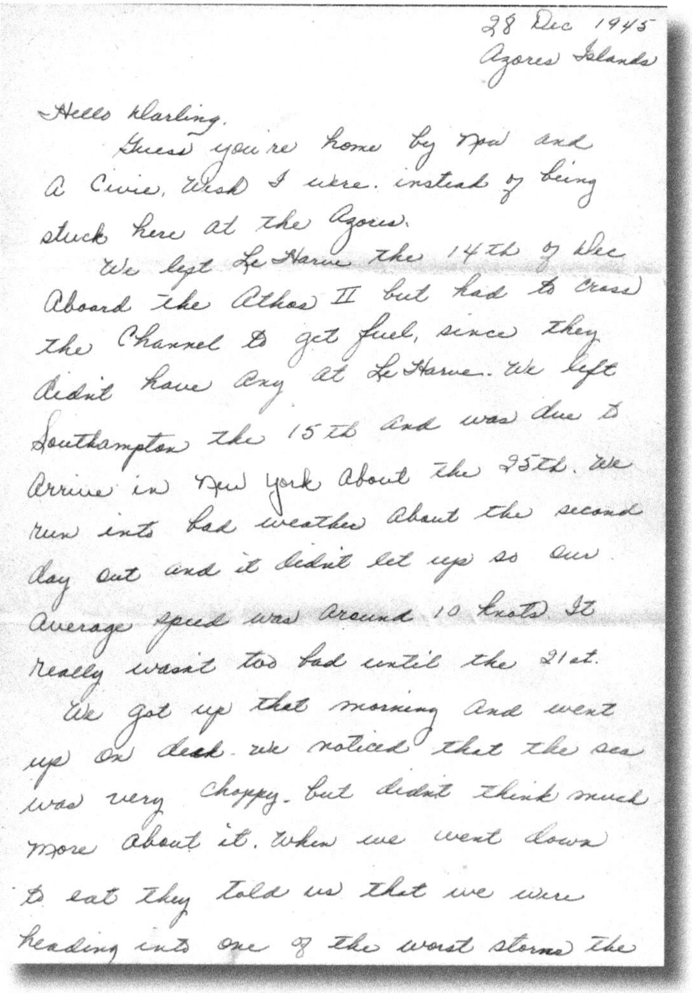

28 Dec 1945
Azores Islands

Hello darling,

Guess you're home by now and a civie, wish I were, instead of being stuck here at the Azores.

We left Le Harve the 14th of Dec aboard the Athos II but had to cross the channel to get fuel, since they didn't have any at Le Harve. We left Southampton the 15th and was due to arrive in New York about the 25th. We run into bad weather about the second day out and it didn't let up so our average speed was around 10 knots It really wasn't too bad until the 21st.

We got up that morning and went up on deck. We noticed that the sea was very choppy. but didn't think much more about it. When we went down to eat they told us that we were heading into one of the worst storms the

First page of letter *

86

Atlantic has seen in the past 35 years. The gale was 78 MPH. That nite it was 110.

At 12:30 Kay Edna & I went up to the lounge to play cards. We had to stop at 1:45 because our cards wouldn't stay on the table and people were flying across the room mixed up with loose furniture. We three sat on the floor and braced ourselves for the worst. Kay was knocked loose and went sailing across the floor she grabbed for the rope they had put up. An the skin was ~~skind~~ skinned back on her hand. We had to stay up there until 3:50 then they told us to put on our life belts and go downstairs. The men made a chain to help us along. They wanted most of the weight on the bottom.

I don't mean to make this sound like it was bad for we weren't the least bit afraid. We stayd down there

Second page of letter *

87

Until 10 that nite. Since the ship wouldn't make it on to n.y. we had to head for the closet land without running into any more storms. That is why we are at the Azores right now. most of the food was ruined and are out of fuel. The ship is pretty well banged up and they are repairing it a little. we have inspectors here and they haven't condemned it or passed it. we have been here since the 25th. And have no idea how much longer we'll stay here. we can't go ashore so have to make the most of ship. There are around 3,000 troops on board. Slim and another one of your boys are here. The 118th Iny div. They don't want us to fratinize with the GI's. They can't come on our deck and we can't go down there on C deck. Well darling I haven't the least idea when I'll get to n.y. for we have to wait for Washington to make

Third page of letter *

up their minds whether to send
another ship after us or to send us
food & medical supplies There were
around 150 injured during the storm
a lot of them have broken bones.
The ships Chaplain is pretty bad off.
They had to give him Blood Transfusions.
But please don't worry darling. I'll
be home someday and we can
pick up where to left off – I love
you very much and I do miss
you somepin awful. I'll sign off
you now – until I reach my I
remain as always.

All my Love.

Bobby –

*Fourth page of letter *

God had a plan for all of us. Little did I know that I would be marrying the girl of my dreams in Reims, France, and honeymooning in the most romantic city, Paris.

Five children, eight grandchildren, and fourteen great-grandchildren later (and still growing) makes me so thankful that God made it all possible.

9

Miscellaneous Information and Pictures About the War

Helen Denton was the personal secretary to General Dwight D. Eisenhower. Mrs. Denton came to our town, Thomson, Georgia, on March 24, 2012, to speak about her experiences during World War II as General Eisenhower's personal secretary. I attended that meeting and was very glad I did. After her talk, I went up to her and told her I was with him and installed his telephone lines in Reims and took care of the war room with the maps at the Little Red Schoolhouse. She told me that she had a picture of the map with the plan for the invasion, and she said she would send it to me. I told her I would send her a picture of Eisenhower holding the pens at the surrender at the Little Red Schoolhouse.

Helen Denton's note *

War Room Picture *

General Dwight D. Eisenhower

The greatest generation, led by General Eisenhower, saved the world from tyranny so that all of us could live in freedom today.

arnold palmer

I have many fond memories of President Dwight D. Eisenhower – but my favorite by far happened on September 10th, 1966. It was my 37th birthday and I was gearing up to play a round of golf when I heard a knock on the door. At first I was annoyed that I had to postpone my game of golf because of some unannounced visitor. But when I went to open the door I received the best birthday gift I could ask for. Standing on my front porch was none other than President Eisenhower. Holding an overnight bag under his arm, he grinned and said, "Say, you wouldn't have room to put up an old man for the night, would you?" We spent the next couple days talking for hours on end. I will always remember that weekend as the best birthday I ever had.

I also had the honor of speaking before a Joint Session of Congress in 1990 to commemorate the 100th birthday of my dear friend, Ike. You probably know President Eisenhower as the man who helped liberate Europe from Hitler's iron grip and establish the U.S. as a post-war leader and beacon of freedom in the world. To me, he was much more than that. He was like a second father to me.

While you and I appreciate the legacy he established as a Five-Star General of World War II and our 34th President, the sad truth is many young Americans today know next to nothing about this American hero, or all the brave men who served with him. I'm pleased to say that since 1945, the Eisenhower Foundation has championed the life, leadership, and character of this great man and continues to play a valuable role in preserving and perpetuating the legacy of President Eisenhower. The work they are doing will ensure that the next generation will not forget one of America's fondest Presidents.

Sincerely,

Arnold Palmer

Arnold Palmer

Arnold Palmer's Letter

Golf was a favorite sport of General Eisenhower.

After the war in France, the French made young French women pay the penalty for having had personal relationships with the Germans. The French civilians in the Montel Mar area of Southern France shaved the women's heads in public as punishment and as a visible sign of collaboration, being a traitor, on August 29, 1944. (In total, 2,315 ladies had their heads shaved.)

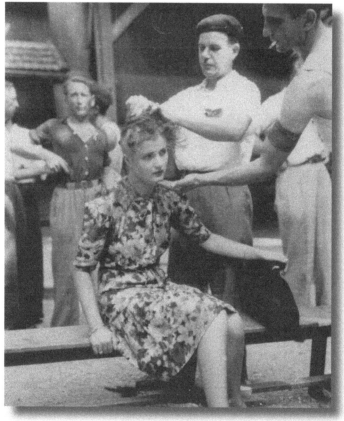

Shaved Head

Colonel Shames

He was the first soldier to be awarded a battlefield commission at Normandy. He was with the 506th PIR, Easy Company, Third Platoon, more notably known as the Band of Brothers. After months of intense training in Toccoa, Georgia, his unit shipped off to England to await the planned invasion of Europe. Their first taste of combat came in the early hours of June 6, 1944—D-Day.

Patton's Picture
General George S. Patton

Seven Famous Patton Quotes to Inspire Young and Old

"By perseverance, study and eternal desire, any man can become great."

"Do everything you ask of those you command."

"If everybody is thinking alike, then somebody isn't thinking."

"May God have mercy upon my enemies, because I won't."

"A man must know his destiny. If he does not recognize it, then he is lost. By this I mean, once, twice, or at the very most, three times, fate will reach out and tap a man on the shoulder. If he has the imagination, he will turn around and fate will point out to him what fork in the road he should take. If he has guts, he will take it."

"Tanks are new and special weapons, -- newer than, as special, and certainly as valuable as the airplane."

"The obvious thing for the cavalryman to do is accept the fighting machine as a partner, and prepare to meet more fully the demands of future warfare."

*Source: The Official General George S. Patton, Jr. website * www.generalpatton.com*

Patton's Quotes

Stalin, Roosevelt, Churchill

These three men, Stalin, FDR, and Churchill, were all allies of WWII who headed up Allied countries during WWII. This picture was taken at the Tehran Conference at the Soviet Embassy, November 21–December 1, 1943.

Americans were given ration books to be able to buy food, gas, household items, etc. It wasn't just hard on us fighting for freedom, but on our loved ones back at home also. Below is a photo of a war ration book.

UNITED STATES OF AMERICA
OFFICE OF PRICE ADMINISTRATION

401383   DW

WAR RATION BOOK No. 3

Void if altered

Identification of person to whom issued: PRINT IN FULL

NOT VALID WITHOUT STAMP

_____
(First name)   (Middle name)   (Last name)

Street number or rural route _____

City or Post Office _____ State _____

AGE	SEX	WEIGHT	HEIGHT	OCCUPATION
		Lbs.	Ft. In.	

SIGNATURE
(Person to whom book is issued. If such person is unable to sign because of age or incapacity, another may sign in his behalf.)

WARNING
This book is the property of the United States Government. It is unlawful to sell it to any other person, or to use it or permit anyone else to use it, except to obtain rationed goods in accordance with regulations of the Office of Price Administration. Any person who finds a lost War Ration Book must return it to the War Price and Rationing Board which issued it. Persons who violate rationing regulations are subject to $10,000 fine or imprisonment, or both.

OPA Form No. R-130

LOCAL BOARD ACTION

Issued by _____
(Local board number)   (Date)

Street address _____

City _____ State _____

(Signature of issuing officer)

War Ration Book *
Front cover

INSTRUCTIONS

1 This book is valuable. Do not lose it.
2 Each stamp authorizes you to purchase rationed goods in the quantities and at the times designated by the Office of Price Administration. Without the stamps you will be unable to purchase those goods.
3 Detailed instructions concerning the use of the book and the stamps will be issued. Watch for those instructions so that you will know how to use your book and stamps. Your Local War Price and Rationing Board can give you full information.
4 Do not throw this book away when all of the stamps have been used, or when the time for their use has expired. You may be required to present this book when you apply for subsequent books.

Rationing is a vital part of your country's war effort. Any attempt to violate the rule is an effort to deny someone his share and will create hardship and help the enemy.

This book is your Government's assurance of your right to buy your fair share of certain goods made scarce by war. Price ceilings have also been established for your protection. Dealers must post these prices conspicuously. Don't pay more.

Give your whole support to rationing and thereby conserve our vital goods. Be guided by the rule:

"If you don't need it, "DON'T BUY IT."

16-32299-1 * U.S. GOVERNMENT PRINTING OFFICE : 1943

Instructions for war ration *
Back cover with instructions

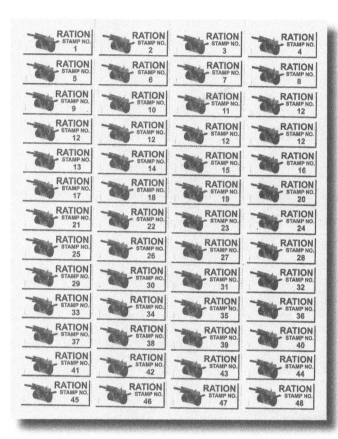

War Ration Stamps *

Ration tickets to buy items

Interesting Facts:

There was never a National Memorial Day parade in Washington, DC, for nearly seventy years until the Veterans Committee said they would sponsor it. This event has become the nation's largest Memorial Day observance.

There was a cemetery site constructed on Omaha Beach. There were white crosses for the American soldiers and black crosses for the German soldiers.

The only Catholic chaplain to die in the Omaha Beach invasion was

Father Ignatius Maternowski.

In my hometown of East Aurora, New York, there were five of us boys who grew up together. One joined the service November 5, 1942, and the other four of us all went into the service on the same day in January 1943. We were all sent to different places. Two of the boys were killed; the first was the first one of us to join, Tech Sergeant Emilio Prisinzano. The second one was Staff Sergeant Joseph Carini, killed in June 1944.

The Buchenwald Complex was one of the largest concentration camps in Nazi Germany, a place of mass murder and slave labor. The camp was liberated by the US Third Army on April 11, 1945. Records say eighty thousand inmates were killed in the camp, but that number could be higher. There were about forty thousand concentration camps throughout Europe.

Men in B Camp
These men were slave laborers in the Buchenwald
concentration camp. Many died from malnutrition.

Bodies

A German girl is overcome as she walks past the exhumed bodies of some of the eight hundred slave workers murdered by SS guards near Namering, Germany. They laid there so that townspeople could view the work of their Nazi leaders.

10

Personal Pictures, Letters, and Commendations

Louis and men with Roosevelt's picture*

I put up the flagpole and built the concrete frame for Roosevelt's picture that one of my men (T/5 Howard Schnebly, the artist) painted while we were in France. I am the first man standing on the left of the picture.

*Parade Picture**
*A parade I was in in Reims, France. I am
the man on the left of the flag.*

Me with my beautiful wife, Bobbie *

Bobbie and me outside the club I built *

Collages of my personal pictures *

Collage #1

Collage #2

Collage #3

My father, Pietro Graziano and my older brother, Carmen *

My mother, Filippa Buscaglia Graziano *

Carmen and Louis *

Louis, Andy, Carmen *

I am pictured with my brother-in-law, Andy Valentino, and my brother, Carmen. We are having a good time in the nightclub I used to come to before I went into the army. It was called the Old Barn.

Believed To Be First

Mrs. Graziano Elected VFW Post Commander

Mrs. Bobbie Graziano is believed to be the first woman ever elected commander of a post in the Veterans of Foreign Wars. She was sworn in as commander of Simon Cason Whaley Post 6672 on Saturday, June 6th.

Mrs. Graziano said, "I know I am the only female in the state of Georgia to hold this post and possibly in the entire nation."

A veteran of World War II with service in France, Mrs. Graziano was sworn in by George C. Pugh (Charlie) of Watkinsville, a past state commander. Pugh had sworn in Mrs. Graziano's husband Louis as post commander in 1964.

Mother of five children and grandmother of three with one expected in October, Mrs. Graziano succeeds Jeffrey Harden as commander of the local post. Mr. Harden has served for the past two years and is returning to the U.S. Navy as a Lt. Commander.

Mrs. Graziano was born in Decatur, Ala. and lived in that state and also in Tennessee while growing up. She had a half brother who served in France during World War I. She met her husband while they were serving in France during World War II. Her son Butch served in the U.S. Marines during the Vietnam war and was wounded.

In August 1943 Mrs. Graziano joined the Women's Army Auxiliary Corp. (WAAC). This branch of service became known later as the Women's Army Corp. (WAC). She was a physical instructor, took her basic training at Daytona, Fla., and spent two years in Sebring, Fla. Her schooling to become a physical instructor was taken in San Antonio, Texas. She was discharged as a staff sergeant.

Mrs. Graziano has been a member of the women's auxiliary of the post for about 20 years, and was president in 1965-66. Last year she served as senior vice commander of the VFW post and received a lifetime membership. Incidentally, there were no females in the VFW until the VFW National Covention in 1978.

Mrs. Graziano hopes to make Simon Casey Whaley Post 6672 one of the best posts in the nation. She said, "to do this will require the cooperation of all the veterans and members of the ladies auxiliary."

Other officers elected were as follows: senior vice commander, Butch Graziano; junior vice, Robert Pounds; quartermaster, Harry Dolyniuk; surgeon, William Lancaster; judge advocate, Bill Shields; chaplain, Jim Grossman; and three year trustee, Roy May

Mrs. Graziano-Charlie Pugh

Bobbie elected post commander

An article in our local newspaper, "The McDuffie Progress"

The Record-Setting

Grazianos

Every member of the VFW can take pride in the Graziano family of Thomson, Ga., whose dedication to veterans is boundless.

Mrs. Bobbie Graziano was selected 1982-83 All American Commander of Georgia's 10th District. Her son, Louis II, earned All American honors as Commander of Post 6672 in Thomson. Mother and son both were feted as All Americans at the 84th National Convention, a VFW first.

The story of the Grazianos begins with Lou Graziano, the father of Louis II and husband of Bobbie.

A native of Buffalo, N.Y., and a World War II veteran of the Battle of the Bulge, he joined Post 6672 in 1962. Three years later he was elected Post Commander. His work for the Post earned him an appointment as National Aide-de-Camp. In 1982, he was named National Aide-de-Camp, Recruiting Class.

Mrs. Graziano, a native of Decatur, Ala., also a World War II veteran, joined the Ladies Auxiliary of Post 6672 and was elected its President in 1966, but she became inactive after her term because of family responsibilities. She joined Post 6672 in 1979 after women were admitted to VFW membership.

From then on, she has done nothing but set records. In 1981, she became the first woman Post Commander in Georgia, the first woman in that Department to be chosen a National Aide-de-Camp, Recruiting Class, and then a member of the All State Team.

With help from her husband and son, she increased the Post's membership from 498 to 633.

In 1982, Bobbie was elected Georgia's first woman District Commander. She became a member of the Century Club, 1982-83. Her District membership jumped from 2,184 to 2,538. Bobbie has been re-elected 10th District Commander for the 1983-84 term. As a 1982-83 District All American Commander, she was the only one from Georgia and the first woman ever awarded this honor. She also had started two new Posts in the 10th District, one while Post Commander and the other this past year as District Commander.

Son Louis, nicknamed Butch, was born in Lackawanna, N.Y., served two tours in Vietnam as a Marine. As a result of being shot nine times, suffering multiple shrapnel wounds and receiving other injuries, he has a 60% disability rating from the VA.

He joined Post 6672 in 1966, but did not become active until 1980, a year after his mother became a member. He served under her as Post Senior Vice Commander in 1981-82. When she moved up to command the 10th District, he succeeded her as Post Commander.

With the help of his parents and friends like Bill Shields, Harry Doylmik, Alton Beard, John Austin, Robert Pounds, Lewis Aldred and Carroll Burton, Commander Butch Graziano increased the Post membership from 633 to 908 during his 1982-83 term. His honors also include two successive years as National Aide-de-Camp, Recruiting Class, 1983 membership in the Century Club and election to the All State Team.

Besides all these distinctions, the Grazianos are the first father, mother and son team of the same Post to sign up 50 new and/or reinstated members in the same year, earning appointments as National Aides-de-Camp, Recruiting Class, the first to receive the Century Club Award for recruiting 100 continuous members each this past year; and the first to have commanded the same Post in Georgia.

Mrs. Graziano is the first woman in Georgia to start two new Posts and possibly the first in the country to do so. Her son received a rotating trophy at the Department Convention for the Post recruiting the most Vietnam veterans, 200.

With people like the Graziano family dedicated to the VFW, the organization is certain to reach Greater Heights.

Louis Graziano II and his mother, Bobbie, were honored at the 84th National Convention as All American Post and District Commanders, respectively. With them is Lou Graziano, father and husband, who started them on their record-breaking ways.

Three GraziZanos

An article in the VFW newsletter about our family's record-setting stats

I am pictured with my son, Louis ("Butch") Charles Graziano, II, and my wife, Bobbie. All three of us served as post commanders for the VFW Post 6672 in Thomson, Georgia.

*Louis in Washington, DC ***

This is a picture of me taken when some of my children, grandchildren, and great-grandchildren took me to Washington, DC, to visit the WWII Memorial. They laughed about Cate, my three-year-old great-granddaughter, and me outwalking them all! (The youngest and the oldest of the group.)

Medals I received:

American Service Medal

European African Medal

Eastern Service Medal

Good Conduct Medal

World War II Victory Medals

Rifle Sharpshooter 171-1943

Battles and Campaigns I engaged in:

Northern France Rhineland

D-Day—Omaha Beach

Battle of the Bulge

US Army Europe/European Theater of Operations

LOUIS C GRAZIANO

To you who answered the call of your country and served in its Armed Forces to bring about the total defeat of the enemy, I extend the heartfelt thanks of a grateful Nation. As one of the Nation's finest, you undertook the most severe task one can be called upon to perform. Because you demonstrated the fortitude, resourcefulness and calm judgment necessary to carry out that task, we now look to you for leadership and example in further exalting our country in peace.

Harry Truman

THE WHITE HOUSE

Harry Truman's Letter *

VETERANS ADMINISTRATION
WASHINGTON 25, D. C.

OFFICE OF
THE ADMINISTRATOR OF
VETERANS AFFAIRS

DEAR FELLOW VETERAN:

I congratulate you upon completion of your service in the armed forces and for your part in bringing to a conclusion a two-front war which resulted in the unconditional surrender of the Axis Powers.

Having been appointed by the President as Administrator of Veterans Affairs, I want to state generally the provisions made by our Government for you and other veterans.

Among the benefits that you may be entitled to are compensation for disabilities, hospitalization, home, farm and business loan guarantee, readjustment allowances, insurance, rehabilitation and vocational training, educational courses, assistance in obtaining employment and provision for your dependents.

Eligibility for each one is dependent upon the facts in the individual case.

If you are interested in any of these provisions, you should write or contact the Veterans Administration office nearest your home. For your convenience, there is, on the reverse of this letter, a list of the Regional Offices with the address of each office.

I feel I should warn you the last deduction for your Government insurance premiums has been made from your service pay. This means from now on you must make these premium payments directly to the Collections division, Veterans Administration, Washington 25, D. C.

DON'T LET YOUR INSURANCE LAPSE! YOU OWE THIS TO YOURSELF AND YOUR FAMILY.

I assure you that the Veterans Administration stands ready to serve you.

Sincerely yours,

Omar N. Bradley

OMAR N. BRADLEY,
General, U. S. Army,
Administrator.

Omar Bradley's Letter *

PAUL C. BROUN, M.D.
10th District, Georgia

COMMITTEE ON
SCIENCE, SPACE, AND TECHNOLOGY
Chairman, Investigations and
Oversight Subcommittee

COMMITTEE ON
HOMELAND SECURITY

COMMITTEE ON
NATURAL RESOURCES

Congress of the United States
House of Representatives
Washington, DC 20515–1010

WASHINGTON OFFICE:
325 Cannon House Office Building
Washington, DC 20515
Phone: (202) 225-4101
Fax: (202) 226-0776

WEB: BROUN.HOUSE.GOV

Dear Mr. Granziano,

It is an honor to extend to you my most heartfelt appreciation on behalf of the American people for your service in World War II. During a time of great turmoil, you bravely fought against fascism and tyranny. You played an integral role in our monumental victory by serving in the 102nd Field Artillery. Without your service, totalitarianism and injustice could have prevailed. Instead, the unity and resolve of our nation and its allies proved insurmountable and the worlds enemies were defeated.

The importance of your service can never be understated. Going to war will always be a terrible endeavor. However, in the words of President Reagan, "there is a difference between the use of force for liberation and the use of force for conquest." You fought to liberate, not to conquer, and you and your family should always be proud of your service to our nation. The victory achieved altered the course of history forever. Now we must ensure that history is never altered to downplay the importance of brave souls like you. I encourage you to tell your story often to our younger generations so that we may never forget the heroic acts of the greatest generation in our history.

We must always be grateful of those who made the ultimate sacrifice in the name of freedom and liberty. For without these heroes, America would not be the greatest country in the World. Furthermore, the example you have given future generations will provide guidance and inspiration for decades to come. The only injustice to possibly come of your service would be for history to erase the memory of your sacrifices. It is of the utmost importance to preserve this history. The WWII memorial will forever stand in remembrance of brave souls like you. It signifies a country delivering freedom and liberty to a continent that was in great peril while saving the lives of millions of people.

Our country is forever indebted to you and your comrades of the 102nd Field Artillery. It is an honor and a privilege to represent you in the U.S House of Representatives. This country is forever grateful for your courageous service and dedication. If I may ever be of service in the future, please don't hesitate to let me know.

May God bless and keep you always,

Thank you for your
service to our nation.
Sempre Si!

Paul C. Broun Jr
Member of Congress

TOCCOA
184 Remsdale Street
Toccoa, GA 30577
Phone: (706) 896-1008
Fax: (706) 896-1009

AUGUSTA
4246 Washington Road
Suite E
Evans, GA 30806
Phone: (706) 442-3857
Fax: (706) 868-8766

ATHENS
3706 Atlanta Highway
Suite 3B
Athens, GA 30606
Phone: (706) 549-9588
Fax: (706) 549-9590

PRINTED ON RECYCLED PAPER

Paul Broun's Letter *

This is the first of the three letters presented to me upon my visit to the WWII monument. A representative arrived to welcome my family and me. I was honored and appreciative of their recognition for my service to my country.

SAXBY CHAMBLISS
GEORGIA

United States Senate
Washington, D. C.
June 2, 2011

Mr. Louis Graziano
236 Hill St.
Thomson, GA 30824

Dear Mr. Graziano:

    I am humbled to have the opportunity to express my most sincere gratitude for you and all the men and women who serve in our military and have sacrificed so much to defend our country's freedom. The sacrifices you made to serve your country during World War II are truly astounding, and every American enjoys freedom today because of your commitment.

    Georgia is a proud military state, and as a member of the Senate Armed Services Committee, I could not be more proud of our military personnel and their dedication to making America safe and secure for our children and grandchildren. I will continue to advocate for the needs of our troops and their families.

    I wish you the best on this special day. If I can ever be of assistance to you in the future, please do not hesitate to let me know.

Very truly yours,

Saxby Chambliss

NOT PRINTED AT GOVERNMENT EXPENSE

Saxby Chambliss's Letter *

JOHNNY ISAKSON
GEORGIA

United States Senate
WASHINGTON, D.C.

June 10, 2011

Mr. Louis Graziano
236 Hill Street
Thomson, Georgia 30824

Dear Mr. Graziano:

It is an honor and a pleasure to send my sincere thanks to you for your service to our great nation. I hope you enjoyed your trip to Washington, D. C. to visit the National World War II Memorial. I am sure your visit brought back many memories of your time in the Army: some good and some very sad. I felt humbled after my visit to this long overdue memorial that honors the 16 million brave men and women who served in the armed forces of the United States, many never returning to their loved ones.

I know this trip meant a lot to you, and I am delighted that your family had an opportunity to accompany you on this journey into your past. I join with them in saying thank you so much for your faithful service to this great country. Without brave soldiers like you who fought during World War II, the citizens of this nation would not enjoy the freedoms which so many take for granted. We owe you a huge debt of gratitude. You are truly a member of the Greatest Generation.

With my warmest personal regards,

Sincerely,

Johnny Isakson

JI/mg

Johnny Isakson's Letter *

Moira Johnson

From:	Rick Tuchscherer - Director, Catholic Social Services [director@cssaugusta.com]
Sent:	Friday, June 06, 2008 1:27 PM
To:	Helen Griffin (E-mail); Robert Rahaim; Vicki Goetz (E-mail); Benjamin Suer; Bill Williams; Bob Kiel; Christopher Pin; David Delabar; Eric Ray; Glenn Yarborough; Hugh Milford; Jacob Almeter; Jacque St. Cyr; Jerry Germann; Joe Almeter; Joe Pretzello; Ken Partridge; Lewis Graziano; Mark R. Lemley; Michael G. Molitor; Rick Tuchscherer; Steven Handlos; Timothy L. McEnery; Tom Schulte; Walter Young

Subject: D-Day

As I look back at this day in history I am grateful for those who stormed the beaches of Normandy to free Europe from the grasp of a demonic man. Many of these Americans, Brits, Canadians, French and other allies gave their lives in this, the largest invasion in history.

I am blessed to have known some of these men who fought for the liberation of others and the preservation of our way of life. My father, who will be 80 years old this August snuck in the Navy at age 15 in 1943. He fought in the battle of the Coral Sea and several others. I am very proud of him. Sir Knight Louis Graziano who is a friend and member of our Knights of Columbus Council at Queen of Angels in Thomson landed on the beaches of Normandy and fought his way across Europe. A good friend of mine Mr. Walter Ehlers, landed on that bloody beach on June 6th and fought as hard as he could. Walter won the Medal of Honor, and is still in demand for speaking engagements. Walt's brother landed on that same beach and was killed in action. We as a nation have been blessed in our history to be able to produce wonderful men of this caliber when we needed them. We need to remember them and honor them. Take a minute out of your day and give thanks that these men saved our freedoms and way of life and freed many millions from the yoke of oppression and evil.

Rick

Rick's email *

This is an email sent to my daughter, Moira, for me.
All my emails come to her, since I don't know anything
about computers. I am thankful I have children
who can take care of all my technical needs.

Certificate for Performance*

Thank you for traveling with me on this journey through my experiences during World War II. I was focused on bringing you these experiences because I felt it was important for others to know the sacrifices that the military men of this country made for the freedom of their loved ones and all Americans.

—Luciano "Louis" Charles Graziano

CPSIA information can be obtained
at www.ICGtesting.com
Printed in the USA
LVHW111023080219
606786LV00001B/1/P